NUTS
COOK
BAG
TAINT
IDIOT
TWAT
DAMN
FELCH

PISS
FLAPS

ASSHOLE

YOU
SUCK

FUCK YOU

EAT SHIT

BITCH

IDIOT

SLUT

COOK
BAG

TWAT

WHORE

WANK

CRAP

BUGGER

TITS

BALLS

PRICK

ARSE

FART

PISS

WANK

CUNT

DAMN

FUCK

BULLSHIT

DICKHEAD

FOOL

MARON

DICKHEAD

GODDAMN

BASTARD

HOOKER

WANKER

TOSSER

SCUMBAG

COCKSUCKER

HOLY SHIT
HOLY SHIT

OH JESUS

FELCH

ASSHAT

TAINT

CUM

PUSSY

JIZZ

TAINT

NUTS

BLOWJOB

SHITHEAD

PRICK

www.ingramcontent.com/pod-product-compliance
Lightning Source LLC
Chambersburg PA
CBHW080828260726

48654CB00027B/1775